If I Lay on my Back I Saw
Nothing but Naked Women

ABOUT THE AUTHOR

Jacqueline Saphra wrote stage plays and screenplays for many years before she rediscovered poetry, her first love. Her pamphlet, *Rock'n'Roll Mamma* from Flarestack, was followed by *The Kitchen of Lovely Contraptions* (flipped eye), which was developed with funding from Arts Council England and nominated for the Aldeburgh First Collection prize. She lives in London and teaches at The Poetry School.

ABOUT THE ILLUSTRATOR

Artist-printmaker Mark Andrew Webber specialises in painstakingly-researched typographic and geometric projects, including his 'Where in the World' series of enormous city maps and 'FORM', a six-part study of line and form. In 2007, Webber was awarded a Silver Cube award from the Art Directors Club of New York. His first solo exhibition, 'Wonderlust', was on display at the Londonewcastle Project Space in London in 2014. He is based in Reading.

If I Lay on my Back I Saw Nothing but Naked Women

Poems by Jacqueline Saphra
Illustrations by Mark Andrew Webber

THE EMMA PRESS

When I was a child I tied my mother and father together with bandages and put a song in their mouths. If I wound them up they sang an Afrikaans duet in perfect thirds. Our house was filled with cookers, stethoscopes, fridges, small hammers and secretaries taking dictation. I sat quietly on an ink blotter while mother plaited my hair and father listened to my heart.

The desk is an heirloom. It's made of imboia. It belonged to my Lithuanian grandfather who used it in his consulting room. He died before I was born. There are secret compartments in the back where I hide problematic words in case I need them later. Sometimes they whisper in the dark. At quiet moments, if I put my ear to the ink blotter, I hear the longer ones mount the shorter ones. Weeks or months later, I catch little phrases or cries coming from inside.

Sometimes my father fell asleep in his study with a cigarette in his hand and set whole books of love poems on fire. My mother suffered from nerves. My father listened regularly to her heart with his stethoscope until he learned to hate its palpitations. He liked to listen to her brain too. He'd warm the end of the stethoscope in hot water then place it on her temple; tell her to think, think hard.

My dark-haired mother was a necromancer. She could vanish whole stories by repeating them over and over until they wore out and fell to pieces. This seemed to make her very tired. While she slept, the stories re-formed themselves and sidled back into her open mouth. The order was never the same twice.

My Australian stepfather stretched his own canvasses. He had a palette made of hardboard and his ancient brushes shed bristles onto the paintwork. One arm was shorter than the other. This was because a funnel-web spider had bitten him when he was a baby. They had operated, but were forced to cut some of the bone away. He'd hold his arms out and show me. *See? One arm is shorter. That's the painting one.*

My first stepmother was blonde and clever. She was on my father's arm when he came to collect me for annual holidays. My two fathers did not dislike each other and sat politely conversing on the sofa; one wielded his stethoscope, the other his paintbrush. It was not entirely clear which of them was in charge.

Sometimes paint spilled and leaked under the door of my stepfather's studio. My mother scrubbed at it with a Brillo pad but the stains were ingrained in the carpet. Not many people bought the paintings so we stacked them in rows four-deep against the walls, which made the rooms considerably smaller. Some we fixed to the ceiling just to get them out of the way. If I lay on my back in bed I saw nothing but naked women.

My father's house had stone floors. My first stepmother felt the cold only in her extremities. Even in the winter she would wander the corridors wearing nothing but gloves and slippers. Sometimes when the doorbell rang she would forget, particularly if she was expecting a parcel. She was on excellent terms with the postman.

My mother began to throw pots. The walls of the kitchen where she worked were studded with small scraps of clay that had spun free of the wheel. The pots would not shape up. She cleared the shelves to make space for various lopsided receptacles and refused to admit their failings. Pouring water at mealtimes from one of my mother's jugs became a daily trial of nerve.

My second stepmother understood about words. She liked some of mine so much she often kept the best ones for herself. Once I caught her pulling a whole string of them out of her sleeve at a dinner party but I didn't let on.

My stepfather worked in oils. Some paints were more costly than others. His favourite was Rose Madder Genuine from the professional range but he would rarely splash out. This was a pity, as it seemed to inspire him. Permanent Rose was a viable alternative although it lacked depth, he complained. It was designed for amateurs.

My mother's tears rolled under my stepfather's piles of paintings and soaked into the frames; this weakened the wood. He left piles of rotted planks when he moved out but he rolled up all the paintings and took them away. My mother abandoned necromancy and took up assertion training.

My second stepmother renounced her dinner parties and took to the law. I would open cupboards on the hunt for jam or clean towels only to discover her secreted inside in the dark, her highlighter pen streaking luminous trails across leather-bound tomes with very small print.

My father took a crash course in Cordon Bleu. He constructed elaborate meals involving spun sugar and truffles and summoned my second stepmother from her studies with the aid of an electronic bell he had purchased for the purpose. She rarely heard it. The food was often cold by the time we ate.

My father's final wife had hair like my mother's. She was partial to muesli, chunky jewellery and modern art. She bagged up all my old words, took them to the charity shop in her rusty Honda and redesigned my father's house around him. He was bemused by her jars of lentils, quinoa, stamps, ginseng tea, wholegrain rice, chick peas and rubber bands. He smoked, dozed, shed his hair and occasionally but inadvertently set fire to unfamiliar designer suites.

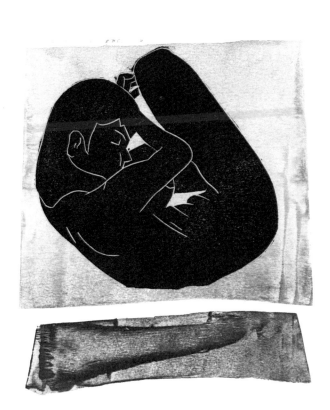

My mother shrank to the size of a small potted plant. The oil paint on the carpet dried into the shape of Africa. She sat in the corner clutching her old skates and dispensing strings of aphorisms on the subject of assertion, the broken record technique and The Swinging Sixties. There were no buttons left on our shirts. Dust lay in drifts on the skirting boards; my mother was too small to keep up with the housework. Needles frightened her.

When I was a child my mother and father lived on different continents. I flew between them. When one was asleep, the other was awake and the telephone rang at all hours. You could never be sure what you heard. Certain phrases were often bent or broken in transit, complete sentences drifted away and were lost in the exchange. Those that arrived intact would generally mutate over time. Airmailed scrawls in permanent ink proved more dependable. Tightly trussed with rubber bands, unable to escape, the words waited immutably in the dark.

ACKNOWLEDGEMENTS

This slow-growing sequence of poems has passed through many hands and I'm thankful to George Szirtes who sowed the seed for it many years ago. Thanks also to all those who helped it along, including Norbert Hirschhorn, Philip Gross, Stephen Knight, Mimi Khalvati and the APW, and the poets of The Vineyard. Thanks to Emma Wright and Rachel Piercey who picked up the poems and ran with them all the way to artist Mark Andrew Webber: my thanks to him too for his intuitively brilliant interpretations. Gratitude, as ever, to my inspirational friends and to my supportive, long-suffering family, and especially to Robin – for everything.

— Jacqueline Saphra

I would like to thank Emma and Jacqueline for letting me be a part of this project. I would also like to thank Suzanne Stallard from Jelly Reading – I would not have been able to create this work without the support of Jelly.

— Mark Andrew Webber

THE EMMA PRESS

small press, big dreams

The Emma Press is an independent publisher dedicated to producing beautiful, engaging and thought-provoking books. It was founded in 2012 in Winnersh, UK, by Emma Wright and the first book was *The Flower and the Plough*, by Rachel Piercey.

Our current publishing programme includes a mixture of themed poetry anthologies and single-author poetry and prose pamphlets, with an ongoing engagement with the works of the Roman poet Ovid.

We publish books which excite us, and we are often on the lookout for new writing. Visit our website and sign up to the Emma Press newsletter to hear about all upcoming calls for submissions as well as our events and publications. You can also purchase our books in our online shop.

http://theemmapress.com

For my mother

THE EMMA PRESS

First published in Great Britain in 2014
by the Emma Press Ltd

Poems copyright © Jacqueline Saphra 2014
Illustrations copyright © Mark Andrew Webber 2014

ISBN 978-1-910139-06-6

A CIP catalogue record of this book
is available from the British Library.

Printed and bound in Great Britain
by Letterworks Ltd, Reading.

theemmapress.com
editor@theemmapress.com